PENELOPE'S

The

Wellbeing

Looking after yourself in a busy world

PENGUIN BOOKS

PENGUIN BOOKS

Published by the Penguin Group

Penguin Books Ltd, 27 Wrights Lane, London W8 5TZ, England

Penguin Putnam Inc., 375 Hudson Street, New York, New York 10014, USA

Penguin Books Australia Ltd, Ringwood, Victoria, Australia

Penguin Books Canada Ltd, 10 Alcorn Avenue, Toronto, Ontario, Canada M4V 3B2

Penguin Books (NZ) Ltd, Private Bag 102902, NSMC, Auckland, New Zealand

Penguin Books Ltd, Registered Offices: Harmondsworth, Middlesex, England

First published by Penguin Books Australia 1998
Published in Penguin Books 1999

10 9 8 7 6 5 4 3 2

Neither the author nor the publisher can be held responsible for claims arising from the mistaken identity of any herbs or vitamins, or the inappropriate use of any remedy or healing regime contained in this book

The moral right of the author has been asserted

Printed in England by William Clowes Ltd

A note from the author

When you see clean, crystal-clear water flowing from a waterfall, you feel swept away by its energy. It is a thing of beauty and you could imagine drinking freely from it. By contrast, a polluted river or pond doesn't contribute to your sense of wellbeing, nor could you ever dream of drinking from its stagnant waters.

Picture your bloodstream in the same manner. When you drink water every day and develop healthy eating habits, oxygen is carried more readily to every cell in your body, your cells are bathed and hydrated, and poisons are removed from your system. Your health and wellbeing are enhanced and your quality of life improved. So drink plenty of water and feed your body only fresh, healthy foods. It's the only way you could hope to cultivate a crystal-clear waterfall in your own body.

Look to your health;
and if you have it . . .
value it next to a good
conscience; for health is
the second blessing that
we mortals are capable
of; a blessing that money
cannot buy.

IZAAK WALTON
(1593–1683)

An apple a day...

There are many delicious apple varieties available at fresh produce markets. Make it a point to try a new variety every week. Apples contain carbohydrate for energy and fibre, and are an excellent source of vitamin C. Remember the old saying . . .

The night-before breakfast

If you haven't got time to make breakfast in the morning, try making it the night before. Pour boiling water over rolled oats or buckwheat or ground wheat in a wide-necked thermos flask. By the morning it will be cooked and still warm.

Develop good drinking habits

To get you into the habit of drinking water, keep a jug of water and a glass beside your bed. Make an effort to drink at least one glass before bed and one glass in the morning. Gradually build this up to two glasses, then three . . .

Arnica —
the wonder plant

Arnica is fabulous for alleviating bruising, shock or trauma after surgery, accidents, falls or sporting injuries. Take five drops in the mouth four times a day until better. Arnica cream is especially effective for clearing bruising, but it should never be used on broken skin.

Record your inspirations

Sometimes a pen and paper aren't at hand and that Important Idea gets lost in the million-and-one things that need doing in a day. Try carrying with you a mini dictaphone or tape recorder to record ideas, meetings and inspirations at any time of the day.

Water while-you-wait

You can never drink enough water, so keep a bottle of filtered water in your car and drink it while you wait at red lights. This is an especially useful health tip for people who spend a lot of time on the road.

Bake to save you time

Slaving over a hot stove keeps
you tied to the kitchen. Consider
baking your meals or simply cooking
your meals slowly on low heat, which
will free you up to do other things
like exercise, helping the children
with their homework, gardening
and reading.

When your period is a pain

When muscle spasms, cramps or headaches get hold of you at that time of the month, place a hot-water bottle or a hot lavender or wheat pack over the area. The heat will improve circulation and relax surrounding muscle fibres.

Feeling stressed
or anxious?

Bach Flower drops (Rescue Remedy)
are great for those times when you
feel stressed or anxious. Take five
drops in the mouth three times a day.
If you've experienced a sudden shock
or a bout of anxiety, take three doses
five minutes apart.

Stock up

We're often tempted to eat takeaway
food because the pantry's empty.
Every month try stocking up on health
foods such as brown rice, cereals,
legumes, dried fruit, seeds, tinned fish
and fruit, jams and nuts. It'll save you
time and ensure you always have
delicious food on hand.

The wonders of green barley powder

Green barley powder is made from the fresh green tip of sprouted barley. It has been found to help the absorption of iron and minerals at a more efficient level, and has been used to fight the growth of cancer cells. Add half a teaspoon to half a glass of juice every day.

Learn to delegate

You can't do everything for everyone.
Learn to delegate responsibility.
Consider which tasks can be allocated
to other people at work or to your
partner or children at home. This isn't
a cop out – it's life.

Red meat alternatives

Don't forget eggs, tofu and legumes are great protein alternatives to red meat. They'll also add variety and interest to your regular meals. Add boiled eggs or cooked legumes to green salad. Or steam tofu for one or two minutes and toss with salad or cooked vegetables.

Ginkgo –
for memory power

Take two Ginkgo biloba tablets a few
hours before an exam or study period,
or even when writing a difficult letter
or essay. This plant increases the
circulation of blood to the brain –
with no side effects – and hence
enhances your concentration and
memory potential.

The humble potato

Don't forget potatoes for a simple
lunch or fast energy fix. Put a large
potato in its jacket into the microwave
oven and cook until tender. Split the
top and fill with salad or beans or
mashed avocado with sea salt.

When you're watching
your weight…

If you're watching your weight but
have to go out for dinner where
low-fat foods aren't likely to be on the
menu, ask the waiter to bring you
freshly squeezed lemon juice to sip,
or four or five slices of fresh orange.
The natural acid from the fruit cuts
through fats and aids digestion.

Restore hormonal balance

Hot flushes, irregular periods and
other menopausal symptoms are all
hormonal imbalances of some kind.
Women with these symptoms or even
women with PMS should take
two capsules a day of the Chinese
herb Dong quai until symptoms
are relieved.

The skin benefits of vitamin E

Vitamin E is a wonder for replenishing dehydrated skin and reducing excessive wrinkles. A water-soluble capsule is the most preferable form. Ask your naturopath to prescribe a dosage that's right for *your* health.

Good scents

Always keep a deodorant and
perfume or aftershave at the office
or in your bag. It can give you an
instant confidence boost, particularly
if you have to be somewhere special
at short notice.

A kind word a day

There are occasions in everyone's life where a kind word has brightened their day. Try to say a kind word each day to your family, colleagues and friends. You may not notice the positive impact, but others will!

Cranberry juice for infection prevention

If you're prone to urinary tract infections, drink a glass of cranberry juice every day. Substances in the cranberry have been found to help prevent these unpleasant infections. Try mixing cranberry juice with your favourite spirit to make a delicious cocktail or pre-dinner drink.

A cure for spring sneezing

If you experience fits of sneezing
in spring, you'll be pleased to know
that relief is at hand. Make a tea
from a herb called golden rod and
drink two or three cups a day.
Or take a garlic and horseradish
tablet after every meal.

Some travel tips

The foods of a particular country are generally suitable for its climate and culture. Therefore try to eat the cuisine of the country you're visiting – provided it's hygienic and safe, of course. Drink only bottled water in eastern countries or travel with a portable water filter.

Musical relief

Music can bring calm and
peacefulness to anxious moments.
And the beauty is, it can travel with
you. If you find music soothing, bring
a walkman with you on public
transport, while waiting in queues or
when you're out walking or jogging.

Think zinc for a healthy prostate

The mineral zinc is essential for the prevention of prostate problems. Ask your naturopath to give you a zinc tally test to obtain your levels of zinc. If the test shows your zinc levels are low, take one zinc tablet after each meal. Have the test again after three months to check your progress.

Quick nausea relief

Ginger has been used in the West for over 2000 years. It has a calming, warming effect on the body and is superb for the relief of travel and morning sickness. If you're feeling nauseous, take one or two capsules of ginger every three or four hours, or sip ginger tea.

The brilliant banana

Bananas are rich in potassium and vitamin C, and are a wonderful – and convenient – source of energy. They're also good for cleansing your bowel. Try to include a banana in your daily fruit intake.

Skip to it!

Increasing your level of fitness can often seem difficult and impractical, but it doesn't have to be. Skipping is one of the quickest ways of getting up your heart rate, and the best thing is, you don't need lots of time, space or expensive clothes and equipment.

Learn a language

Being able to speak a language other than your own is a skill well worth cultivating. Choose a language that you like and take up a beginner's course, or learn the language of the country you're about to visit and practise while you're there.

Instant airconditioning

If you don't have airconditioning in
your car, don't despair. Place an
icepack or a block of ice in an ice
chest in the back seat of your car.
Leave the lid off. The ice will
gradually cool the air, which will
make those long, balmy
drives bearable.

Oatmeal for itching relief

If you suffer from dermatitis, psoriasis or eczema, place one cup of oatmeal in a knotted stocking or gauze or muslin bag, and lower it into a warm bath. Bathe yourself in the water and gently towel dry. The oatmeal's soothing anti-inflammatory properties will reduce itching.

Simple soup snacks

To satisfy your urge for a snack, pour
some homemade soup into ice-cube
trays and freeze. When needed,
take out a few from the freezer, pour
a little boiling water over the top
and enjoy. Simple!

A tip for shiny hair

For really shiny hair, rinse your hair with a mixture of one teaspoon of soda to a cup of warm water. (This tip works best if you still have hair spray in your hair.) The results will surprise you.

'Must-go' dinners

On Friday evenings, Canadians in Nova Scotia traditionally enjoy 'must-go' dinners. 'Must-go' dinners are made from all the leftovers in the fridge. The results are creative and the practice ensures there's no waste. Try it yourself.

Protect yourself
with garlic

Garlic is a popular herbal remedy
which is best known for its
treatment of coughs and colds.
To protect yourself from bacterial
problems – especially when you're
travelling – take a garlic capsule
after each meal.

Bathtime bliss

Treat yourself to a long and
luxuriating bath once a week.
Make it a truly pampering experience
by softening the water with half a
cup of soda and then adding a few
drops of lavender oil. The lavender
fragrance will linger in your
bathroom for hours.

Keep copies of
your documents

For peace of mind, photocopy your
address book as well as the cards in
your wallet. It'll save you lots of
hassles if you misplace your wallet or
address book, or indeed if they're
stolen. It's always a good idea to do
this if you're about to travel.

Carrot juice –
the elixir of life

Try drinking a glass of carrot juice
every day. Carrots are filled with
natural enzymes and beta carotene,
which can help the body resist
diseases such as cancer and
cardiovascular disease.

Gifts for
new-found friends

When you're about to travel, it's a
nice idea to buy a few small gifts or
souvenirs to take with you on your
trip. These gifts are great for saying
'thank you' and even 'goodbye' to
new-found travelling friends. It's a
simple gesture that can give a
tremendous thrill.

Mobile hot food

Use a thermos flask to carry hot soup, herbal tea or even a vegetable casserole to work. The food or drink will stay hot, so you won't need a microwave oven to heat it up.

Time to take
your vitamins

Due to their concentration, vitamins
taken on an empty stomach can
cause stomach pain. Ideally, energy
vitamins such as Bs, Cs and Es should
be taken after breakfast; relaxing
vitamins such as calcium should be
taken after dinner.

The one-day inner-body cleanser

Sometimes your body needs a complete break from solid foods. Choose a suitable weekday or perhaps a weekend, and drink a large glass of fresh fruit juice every two hours. You'll clear poisons and wastes from your body and feel fabulously invigorated.

Bilberry — for better vision

Substances in the bilberry plant can help combat night blindness. In fact, RAF pilots during World War Two improved their night vision by eating bilberry jam. Take one teaspoon of bilberry tincture every morning, but do see your naturopath for a dosage that's right for you.

A time-saving hair tip

To save time waiting for hair treatments and protein packs to take effect, rub them into your hair before you exercise. The treatment will work as you work out, so you'll need only to rinse your hair in your own good time!

Feet fitness

While talking on the phone, take off
your shoes and stretch your feet.
A common yoga stretch is to lift your
toes up and down ten times, and then
to stretch your toes outwards ten
times. See if you can lift only your
big toe up and down while you hold
down your other toes.

For fresh breath

For long-lasting fresh breath and sparkling teeth, keep a toothbrush and toothpaste handy and brush after every meal. Floss regularly, as the build-up of food debris can also contribute to bad breath. These are simple tips, but they're so often overlooked.

If takeaway is a must...

Discover the healthiest takeaway food outlet in your area; that is, one that prepares food using a range of vegetables and minimal fat. Avoid creamy sauces and fatty meats, and consider lighter vegetarian dishes for dinner.

Relax with lavender

Lavender is highly regarded as a calming herb. If you're tired and stressed or you've been crying, place a small moist lavender bag over your eyes. Relax like this until you feel settled and refreshed.

Reclaim your precious time

Why not arrange for someone else
to do those annoying chores that
eat away at your precious time?
It doesn't cost much for someone
to hand-wash your car or do a few
hours' ironing, and it'll leave you
free to catch up with other more
important tasks.

To soothe sore eyes...

The herb eyebright is wonderful for soothing irritated or mildly infected eyes, and 'allergy eyes'. Add one teaspoon of eyebright to one cup of boiling water. Allow to cool, then strain. Use an eyebath to bathe your eyes with the 'tea' every night until better.

Get organised!

Loose pieces of paper get lost and forgotten. Buy yourself a diary or an organiser and get into the habit of keeping your messages, appointments and thoughts together. Take it with you wherever you go. Good habits create good thinkers.

A word on premature ejaculation

Look closely at your health, and your fitness and stress levels, if you have this problem. Cut out all stimulants such as caffeine, cola drinks and alcohol, and watch your use of sleeping or headache pills. Exercise, drink plenty of water, meditate and go easy on yourself.

Bored with sandwiches?

When sandwiches are no longer
whetting your appetite, place a
range of fillings in a takeaway dish
and eat them with a fork. Experiment
with different ingredients: tuna,
baby beets, eggs, avocado, rice
salad, salmon, tomato, cucumber,
rocket lettuce, alfalfa . . .

To relieve
neck tension...

When you feel your neck muscles
stiffening, roll your head around in
a clockwise motion two or three
times. Then repeat the action
anticlockwise. You'll feel the tension
melt away, and you can do it at any
time, in any place.

A memory tip
for older people

As you get older, your short-term
memory can deteriorate. It doesn't
help that older people tend to drink
more coffee and tea, which dehydrate
the brain. Drink more water. It
rehydrates your brain and will improve
your memory over time.

Feeling down?

Sometimes all you need to lift
you from that 'flat' feeling is a
distraction. Visit a friend or hire
a favourite movie. Go shopping or
play a video game – do anything
as long as your mind is active
and preoccupied.

Three meals a day

Just as a car needs petrol to keep going, your body needs food – at least three meals a day. Food provides essential vitamins and minerals and keeps up your energy levels. And contrary to popular perception, you don't lose weight by skipping meals.

Try organic wines

Did you know that the histamines and additives in some wines can cause hayfever-like symptoms? If you suffer from allergies, try organic wines; they're much easier on the system. Keep a few bottles on hand for when allergy season aggravates your hayfever.

Boost your immune system

Before and during winter boost your immune system with the help of the herbs echinacea and astragalus. Ask your naturopath for a formula or take one tablet of each herb once a day after food.

Take time out

Try to set aside fifteen minutes in
your day to ring loved ones and
friends. Free your mind from home
and work worries for that period
of time and arrange your social life,
enquire about holidays and keep
up with old friends and family.

Move that body!

If your job requires you to sit for
most of the day, make an effort to walk
around the office every half hour.
This will refresh your mind as well
as relieve congestion and poor
circulation in the buttock area.
You could even do ten to twenty
squats to boost circulation.

Nutritious spreads for quick snacks

Peanut butter, and cashew and tahini (sesame seed) spreads are nutritious and protein-rich. For a protein snack, try one of these spreads on bread. Children will enjoy them too. You might like to drizzle some honey over the top.

Posture problems

Poor posture can create all sorts of neck and back problems, especially in later life. Take positive steps to improve your posture *now*. Always be aware of how you hold yourself whenever and wherever you are so that good posture becomes a habit.

Hands tell all

The first part of your body to reveal
your age is actually not your face –
it's your hands. Keep a tube of hand
cream beside your bed or in your
bag, briefcase or office drawer and
use it regularly. If you suffer from
any form of dermatitis, use
sorbolene cream before bed.

Colour your thoughts

Whenever you feel stressed, take
a few minutes to think of a
relaxing colour such as pale blue,
white, mauve or green. Bathe yourself
in this colour in your mind and then
tackle your stress. See how much
calmer you feel.

A bowl of goodness

If you need to be reminded to eat
more fruit, keep a bowl of fresh fruit
in a place where you can see it at
home or at work. Eat one or two
pieces between meals or just when
you feel you need a snack.
Experiment with unusual and
exotic fruits.

The advantages of
white wine

When you're eating a meal high in
protein such as meat, fish or beans,
sip on a glass of white wine. The acid
in the wine assists the breakdown of
protein in the stomach and acts just
like hydrochloric acid, which is
produced naturally in the stomach
to break down protein.

No-pill headache relief

The essential oils of rosemary and peppermint have been found to help relieve certain types of headaches. Keep a small bottle of each oil and either sniff them both regularly or place one drop of each into your nostril every hour.

A natural laxative

Apples are great for relieving
constipation. The pectin in apples
acts as a natural laxative without
giving you sudden diarrhoea or wind.
If you're constipated, eat an apple –
with its skin on.

Folate — a must for mothers-to-be

Folate is a B-group vitamin found in green vegetables, wholegrain breads and cereals, and dried beans. To reduce your chances of having a baby with spina bifida, increase your intake of folate at least one month before pregnancy and for the first three months of pregnancy.

For strong
hair and nails...

Kelp is a seaweed derivative that's high in minerals, which is great for strengthening hair and nails. Sprinkle half a teaspoon of kelp powder on your salads daily and you'll soon notice a positive change.

The couscous alternative

Couscous is a nutritious grain
made from semolina. Its small,
cream-coloured pellets make a delicate
base for any dish. It's a fabulous
alternative to rice, and is easy for
children and older people to digest.
The next time you make a rice dish,
use couscous instead.

Have you heard of phytoestrogens?

Phytoestrogens are natural plant oestrogens that can help alleviate the symptoms of menopause. Organic soymilk and soy products contain phytoestrogens, so try to include soymilk and soy products in your daily diet.

Take stock of your life

Are you doing what you really want
to be doing in your life? If the
answer is 'no', make a list of the
ways in which you can change the
situation. No matter how long it takes,
work through that list until you're
finally doing what you've always
dreamed of doing.

Food combining

To take the load off your digestive system and improve your metabolism, follow the rules of food combining. Try not to eat protein (meats, nuts, dairy products) with starches (potatoes, beans, grains), and eat fruit by itself.

Go herbal

Too much caffeine can cause serious
health problems, including high blood
pressure and digestive disorders.
Herbal teas are caffeine-free and
come in a wide range of flavours.
Do your body a favour and each day
substitute a cup of coffee or tea with
a cup of organic herbal tea.

A stress-free start

Have your packed bags ready at the
front door the night before you go on
holidays or fly out on a work trip.
It really does make for a smooth
and stress-free start. It'll also give
you time to sit down and enjoy a
good breakfast.

Talk s-l-o-w-l-y

Make a conscious effort to talk
more slowly than usual. This
automatically slows down your
breathing and heart rate, and also
allows you to clear your head and
clarify your thoughts.

Lose that 'tube'

No matter what your age, it's never too late to lose that extra 'tube' around your waist. Avoid beer and wine for six weeks, replacing them with mineral water with a touch of lime, vodka and tonic or Campari and soda.

Choose wisely

Even when you're eating on the run, choose foods with the lowest fat content. For example, have your fish grilled instead of battered, your chips baked instead of fried, your pasta sauces tomato-based instead of cream-based. Choose juices or water instead of soft drinks.

For that true tea taste...

For quality black and herbal teas at work or at home, use a tea ball and tea leaves. Tea prepared from leaves tastes better and is better for you because pure tea leaves retain their natural oils and hence improve the quality of the tea you drink.

Empty your brain

Just like a garbage bin, the brain can
overflow with unwanted 'rubbish'.
Make an effort to empty your brain of
all thoughts for five minutes three
times a day. Visualise travelling
through a white tunnel in which you
leave behind all your unwanted
thoughts and feelings.

Marvellous miso

Miso is a fermented soybean paste that's full of protein and minerals. It's made in Japan and has a lovely nutty aroma and taste. For a delicious soup, pour a cup of boiling water over one teaspoon of miso paste, but watch your intake as it's relatively high in salt.

Cotton is best

If you're prone to allergies or you
suffer from asthma, hayfever or sinus
problems, never use tissues or
handkerchiefs made from synthetic
fabrics. Use only cotton handkerchiefs
as the natural fibre won't cause you
any irritation.

Feeling sluggish?

For instant relief from lethargy and sluggishness, close your eyes and take five deep breaths every hour. You'll feel strangely energised and calm.

A natural cleanser

Commercial cleansers are often harsh
and drying on your skin, not to
mention expensive! Almond oil is a
natural cleanser and makeup remover
that's gentle even on sensitive skins.
It leaves skin feeling clean and soft.
Give it a try.

Peppermint tea for indigestion relief

If you suffer from indigestion, drink three or four cups of organic peppermint tea a day. The essential oil contained in peppermint leaves settles the gall bladder and helps to relieve that bloated, 'burpy' feeling after a fatty meal.

There's nothing like a good joke

The act of laughing releases
endorphins and enkephalins –
hormones that make you feel great.
Cut out your favourite jokes from
books, newspapers or magazines
and keep a few at work, at home or
even in the car. Share them with
friends and spread the cheer.

Keep in touch

Sometimes keeping in touch with
friends interstate or abroad can seem
all too hard. A phone call isn't
always practical and letters can take
too long to write. Buy a stack of
postcards and send one regularly to
your friends. It'll make keeping in
touch so much easier.

Calm by candlelight

Candlelight sets the tone for a spell of
relaxation. Light your candles, play
your favourite music, turn off the
lights and sink into an armchair.
The soft, flickering candlelight
is immediately calming.

For those 'weepy' times...

If you become weepy, sensitive or moody at that time of the month, suffer through it no longer. Ask your naturopath for a herb called pulsatilla and feel 'normal' again!

Raise the count

The cause of men's low sperm count
isn't really known but scientific
research suggests a healthier lifestyle
and a herb called schisandra may help.
If your sperm count is low, watch
your diet, try to exercise regularly
and take one or two tablets of
schisandra a day.

Sleep tight

As the demands on our waking lives increase considerably, so too does the need for quality sleep. Try getting eight hours' sleep a night – even for one week – and see how both your energy levels and your ability to deal with stress improve.

Information squeeze

Broaden your knowledge or 'read'
that book you've always wanted to
by listening to a talking book or even
a lecture tape while you drive. You
can squeeze in a lot of information
in this way – without
any effort!

A day of rest

Set aside one day a week in which
you're not madly rushing from place to
place. Relax and unwind on this day;
hibernate if you wish! Take the phone
off the hook or put on the answering
machine, and say 'no' to functions.
Make this *your* day.

Exfoliate for glowing skin

If your skin looks dull and dry, give it a 'cut and polish' by exfoliating with a skin brush or loofah. If using a skin brush, keep your strokes upward, long and light; if using a loofah, keep them gentle and circular. Follow up with a rich moisturiser and your skin will thank you!

A computer hazard

Staring at computer screens for much of the day can cause eye strain and vision problems. It's important to give your eyes a break regularly, even for a few seconds every five minutes or so. Ideally you should try to look into the distance. Use lubricating eye drops if your eyes feel dry.

Comfort treats

Many people eat for emotional rather than physical reasons, with devastating consequences for their health, weight and self-esteem. Instead of buying junk food to comfort you and help you escape, buy yourself a magazine, a book, a piece of clothing or a video game.

The medicinal effects of mushrooms

The Chinese and Japanese have for many centuries known of the medicinal effects of mushrooms. Incorporate shiitake mushrooms into your diet to boost your immune system, normalise your bodily functions and help fight tumors and cancers.

Set your goals – now!

You shouldn't wait for New Year's Eve
to establish yourself a set of goals.
Start right now – and don't forget
to write them down. If one of your
goals is to improve your wellbeing,
begin by practising six health hints
in this book.

Protection for your liver

The plant St Mary's thistle has been
found to have substances that protect
the liver against pesticides, household
chemicals, pollution and alcohol,
and also help to lower cholesterol.
Take one tablet or drink one cup of
St Mary's thistle tea daily.

A fuss-free meal

When 'simple' is the word of the day,
chop up some vegetables such as
potatoes, pumpkin, broccoli, zucchini
and cauliflower. Cover with two or
three cups of water, two tablespoons of
honey and a dash of soy sauce, and
bake at 250°C for one hour. Easy!

Bitters –
for alcohol control

Drink bitters, lime and soda when
you need to watch your alcohol
intake at parties or social gatherings.
The bitters assists digestion, which
will help you to feel well the next day,
and because there's no alcohol you'll
avoid a dreadful hangover.

Don't be so sweet!

Make an effort to reduce the amount of refined sugar you add to your tea and coffee. It not only causes tissue damage but it also disrupts your metabolism and arterial system, causing long-term fatigue, diabetes, indigestion, and pain and discomfort to arthritic joints.

A natural cure for warts

Having warts burnt off doesn't always
have curative results, so try taking
thirty drops of thuja tincture in a glass
of water for two to three months.
It has the effect of killing the wart
virus, causing the wart to fall off in its
own time. Consult your naturopath
before treating children's warts.

To prevent migraine...

The herb feverfew was widely used as
a remedy for migraine by the ancient
Greeks, and is still useful in
preventing migraine attacks,
headaches and menstrual cramps.
If you suffer from any of these, take
one capsule after every meal at the
onset of symptoms.

Your car, your haven

Look upon your car as a safe haven,
a place you can enjoy being by
yourself. If you know you're in for
'one of those days', play your favourite
CD or cassette in your car as you
travel to work.

Fatty foods and
your gall bladder

If you tend to feel nauseous or bilious
after eating fatty foods, you may have
a problem with your gall bladder.
Ask your naturopath for a tea made
from either the fringe tree or barberry
herb and drink one cup after meals.
Ideally, try to stay away from fatty
foods altogether!

A miracle herb
for depression

St John's wort is a herb that has been
considerably successful in treating
depression and anxiety, especially
where the immune system has
been lowered after glandular fever,
for example, or a severe flu.
Take one tablet or have one cup
of tea three times a day.

All about iron

Iron carries oxygen throughout the body, fights infection and produces energy from the food we eat. If you're low in iron, eat more lean meats or add vitamin-C-rich foods (broccoli, capsicum, citrus fruits) to your vegetarian meals as this will improve your absorption of iron.

A must-have for the home or work office

Orthopaedic office chairs aren't a luxury – they're vital to helping you maintain good posture and hence spinal health. Orthopaedic chairs are a must for people whose work demands they spend long periods of time sitting, whether in a home or work office.

Junk food

Remember: junk food means junk health, junk weight, junk energy. Change your eating habits – today!

Help for hypertension

If you suffer from hypertension, drink
hawthorn berry tea three times a day,
or take two or three capsules daily.
In addition, take one magnesium tablet
every day. Both are fabulous 'tonics'
for the heart.

Good drinking habits for children

Encourage your children to drink lots of water every day and experiment with refreshing teas such as cold mint tea or iced lemongrass tea. All this will help to prevent urinary tract infections, which often go undiagnosed in children.

Nutty treats

Buy a variety of nuts such as pistachios, almonds and walnuts and eat them any time you feel peckish. They're not only delicious but they also contain quality protein and monounsaturated fats, which are necessary for healthy skin.

Are you getting enough?

. . . Greens, that is! Spirulina is a sea
protein that is high in chlorophyll.
If you're not eating something green
every day, try taking one or two tablets
of spirulina daily or sprinkle a
teaspoon of the powder onto your
food. Spirulina helps to repair cells
and is a great blood cleanser.

Black tea and kidney stones

Black tea – strong, brewed black tea in particular – has a high concentration of oxalate, which is the primary component of kidney stones. If you drink a lot of black tea, make the switch to herbal teas, which have a low oxalate component. (And drink lots of fresh water too.)

A sweet remedy for allergy sufferers

If you suffer a runny nose and watery eyes during allergy season, chew on a small piece of honeycomb between meals. The propolis content in honeycomb and the antibacterial effects of honey reduce the histamine reaction in your body and can help relieve these allergy symptoms.

Solutions for sensitive skin

Prevent irritation to sensitive skin by wearing cotton clothes that have been washed in a mild soap and rinsed thoroughly; wear cotton-lined rubber gloves when working with detergents; and keep your fingernails short to reduce damage to your skin when the urge to scratch is too great.

Feeling 'strung out'?

Nutmeg is a warming spice great for settling the nerves at those times when you feel 'strung out'. Add half a teaspoon of nutmeg to half a glass of warm water. It can make you forget your problems for a short time and give you a sense of quietness and euphoria.

Protect yourself
against flu

Two or three months before flu
season is the best time to work at
preventing the flu. Take one garlic
capsule daily and drink fresh citrus
juices such as grapefruit, lemon and
orange juice. And keep warm to
prevent catching a chill.

Stimulate your sex life

Jasmine oil is highly respected
in India as a sexual stimulant.
Massage some jasmine-based massage
oil into your body, especially in the
abdomen and groin areas.
Alternatively you could burn some
of the oil in an oil burner or even
drink jasmine tea.

Raw energy

Try eating raw foods one day a week.
This can include sliced raw fruit and
vegetables, and vegetable juices.
Raw foods help to clean the bowel
and give you 'enzyme energy'.
Enzymes are 'living' proteins that help
to stimulate your digestive juices.

Spice up your cereal

Eating cereal for breakfast is a great
way to start the day, but if you find
you need a bit of variety try livening
up your breakfast cereal or oat
porridge by adding a little pure
vanilla, some pure maple syrup,
a dash of cardamom and any
fruit you like.

Ginger –
the warming herb

Ginger is a warming herb that
stimulates the circulatory system
and can prevent sudden illness.
In Chinese medicine heat is life, hence
ginger is greatly esteemed as a 'giver
of life'. So when travelling from hot to
cold climates, take two or three
capsules of ginger a day.

For extra strength...

In ancient times, gladiators ate barley and wheat to strengthen their bodies before battle. Strengthen your body by doing the same. Both grains are loaded with vital nutrients and can be found in breads and cereals, and added to soups, casseroles, breads, pancakes and salads.

It won't happen overnight...

A flat stomach doesn't just happen – for either men or women; you have to work at it daily. Start with fifty stomach crunches a day, then work your way up. As you're doing your crunches, concentrate on your abdominal muscles so that you avoid using your neck and causing injury.

The dreaded 'H'

If you suffer outbreaks of herpes,
take one tablet of the amino acid
lysine every day. In addition to this,
avoid foods that contain L-arginine,
especially nuts and chocolate but also
rye, corn and gelatine.

A must for every woman

Check your breasts immediately after your period has finished. Raise your arm, and with a flat hand feel the breast using a circular motion. Feel under the armpit also, then repeat on the other side. See your doctor if you detect anything unusual.

Embark on a
reading adventure

Ask your friends or local bookseller to
recommend a good book and get into
the habit of reading every night – even
if it's just a few pages. You might also
like to join a reading group or book
club and share your reading
adventures with others.

Know your first aid

Many people talk about learning first aid but never seem to get around to doing it. Take the time to learn basic first aid *now* and keep a book and kit on hand in the house and in the car. This is particularly important if you have a family.

Snack suggestions

For a quick energy snack, make a topping by mixing salmon or tuna with diced tomato and onion, and a dash of paprika or chilli sauce. Or make a spread with mashed avocado, diced tomato and some chilli sauce. Spoon or spread onto a slice of bread or toast or dry biscuit.

Focus on footwear

While you might feel that you don't need the latest 'high-tech' runners, don't forgo good foot care. Ask for help to find the best sports shoe for your type of foot, lifestyle and recreation, and look after the most neglected part of your body – your feet.

Flatulence control

Charcoal absorbs a range of chemicals and toxins and is useful if you suffer flatulence or constipation after eating. Start by taking half a charcoal tablet after every meal. Halve the dosage when the symptoms subside a little and then use only when needed.

A health tip for smokers

Smokers should increase their daily intake of vitamin C as every cigarette extracts 20–30 mg of vitamin C from the body. Eat plenty of citrus fruits, strawberries, cabbage, cauliflower and other vitamin-C-rich foods to help guard against the damaging effects of nicotine on cell tissue.

Heat therapy

To relieve aching tight muscles or
even to relax before bed, stand under
a hot shower for a few minutes.
While your skin is still warm, rub
in some body lotion which could
contain the warming and relaxing
essential oils of lavender
and rosemary.

Potato water for an acidic stomach

If you suffer the discomfort of an acidic stomach, make sure you eat boiled potatoes and drink the water regularly. Even simply eating more potatoes can help. Potatoes are an antacid whose carbohydrate content soothes that sickly acid feeling.

A late-afternoon freshener

Around the late afternoon many
people find their breath becomes stale,
especially people who over-stimulate
their saliva by talking a lot! If you
find this happening, try chewing some
medicated gum, which helps fight
plaque and is both sugarless and
virtually flavourless.

Weekend lunch-making

On weekends make some nourishing
sandwiches with wholemeal bread,
curried egg, chicken, tahini paste
or even tinned fish. Or make a
large pot of minestrone soup and
divide it into single-serve containers.
Freeze and use as you please for
lunches on the go.

Flower power

We give flowers to celebrate or commiserate in a wide range of situations. Flowers express our love, gratitude, concern and sorrow without our ever needing to say a word. Make someone you love or care about happy and send them flowers. You can't go wrong.

A word on essential oils

Essential oils can be harmful if used incorrectly. Never take essential oils *internally* or use undiluted on your skin without professional direction. Do your body a favour and choose only pure, natural (not synthetic) essential oils as they vary markedly in purity and effectiveness.

Cuticle care

While soaking in the bath, treat your nails to some conditioning by rubbing lanolin cream into your cuticles. Wash away the lanolin before you step out. Your nails and cuticles will become stronger and healthier, especially if you do this regularly.

Vary your vegetables

Vegetables can become bland if you eat the same vegetables cooked in the same way day in, day out. Try adding a range of chopped vegetables to pasta sauces, soups, rissoles, meat loaf, lasagne, omelettes and casseroles, or simply mash them with a dash of milk and sea salt.

A herbal skin healer

Goldenseal and echinacea powders
make a magnificent healer of old
sores, ulcers or slow-healing wounds.
Take a pinch of each powder and
sprinkle on twice a day.

Do your eyes a favour

Invest in a pair of sunglasses with optimum ultraviolet protection, even if you have to pay a little more. The money will be well spent, as the sun can do serious damage to your eyes. You might like to ask your optometrist for advice.

Gout and
rheumatism relief

Nettle is helpful in relieving the
symptoms of gout and rheumatism.
Drink nettle tea three times a day.
In addition to this, make a foot bath
regularly by adding two cups of nettle
tea and one tablespoon of Epsom salts
to one litre of warm water.

Are you lactase deficient?

If you're lactase deficient (lactose intolerant), don't immediately assume that you must avoid all dairy products. Most people with a lactase deficiency can still digest some lactose – the equivalent of a standard glass of milk – without any problem. Just watch the size of your servings.

Winners and losers

Remember these sage words: 'A loser sees a problem in every answer. A winner sees an answer in every problem'. Be a winner!

Fragrant feet

For pleasant-smelling feet shake a few drops of essential oil of rosemary and peppermint into the soles of your shoes every day.

A tip for heart health

Monounsaturated fats reduce blood cholesterol and hence the potential for heart disease. These 'good' fats are found in salmon oil, linseed oil, cold-pressed oil, canola oil and olive oil. For good heart health, avoid heating these oils as their value is lost in the heating process.

Take the time to plan

We spend days planning a holiday but often waste our precious weekends through a complete lack of thought. Take the time to plan your weekends. Keep an updated list of people to catch up with or movies to see or places to visit so that you're never short of ideas.

Restore old friendships

Growing apart from friends is just
a part of life, but some friendships
are worth restoring. Usually it takes
only one of you to break the ice.
Gather the courage to ring an
old friend and take the first step
towards what could become a great
friendship once more.

The key to wellbeing

Good health and wellbeing are all
about making small changes to your
diet, attitude and daily routine and
practising them until they become
habits. It's not always easy, and you
need to take small steps slowly rather
than one giant leap. But be patient:
the rewards are waiting for you.

About the author

Penelope Sach is a practitioner
of naturopathic and herbal medicine,
and runs a private practice in
Woollahra, Sydney, Australia.
Recognising the need for high-quality
fluids, she developed a range
of organically-grown herbal teas,
which have become increasingly
popular in Australia and more
recently in Asia. Penelope is also the
author of *On Tea and Healthy Living*
and *Take Care of Yourself*.